A Chauvinist is...

by Marcella Markham
with cartoons by
Dominic Poelsma

Happy Christmas !

✗

EXLEY PUBLICATIONS

By the same creative team:
Old is . . . great!

© Marcella Markham (text)
© Dominic Poelsma (illustrations)

First published 1979 by Exley Publications Ltd, 12 Ye
Corner, Chalk Hill, Watford, Herts, United Kingdom
WD1 4BS.

First printing August 1979
Second printing February 1981
Third printing May 1982

ISBN 0 905521 30 7 (hardback)
ISBN 0 905521 32 3 (paperback)

Photograph of Dominic Poelsma by Carolyn Johns

Printed by Kossuth Printing House, Budapest.

Preface

There are approximately 150 members of the United Nations and I've done my bit towards international cooperation by marrying a good cross-section of them. So I am now in a position to assure you that a chauvinist is a chauvinist the world over. Cochon, porco, schwein or pig!

I may be wrong but I don't think chauvinists are found under toadstools. They are created. We create them. Maybe there is a little seed of chauvinism in every child just waiting to be given manure, and we sure supply it. By the bucket! The least aware of us create them then step back in horror at the monsters we fashioned into sons and lovers and husbands. We shouldn't complain. We should have our heads examined!

I care about people and have a large capacity to love and show it. I kiss friendly men, women, children, dogs and pussy cats. The only trouble is that this impulse has often been misunderstood by men and women. The men who have misunderstood a moment of love and affection have been frightened by it. The word 'commitment' or 'sex' leaps into their heads. These are chauvinists who ridiculously and sadly deprive themselves of affection, fun and warmth. Chauvinists are buttoned-up people who can't share momentary joy.

I once kissed a woman and she said, 'Don't kiss me. I am not woman oriented.' I thought 'How sad. She has cut out half the population of the world.' I'm certain that we destroy the time we have by role playing and being frightened by each other. If we dropped the poses and thought of each other as vulnerable humans in our relationships, we would have such joy. We think we have progressed. But, it hasn't been much. The only revolution has been the scientific one – the pill. That's the only liberation, the sexual one. The little pill which made us advance below the belly must graduate to our minds and create an emotional revolution of responsibility towards each other.

These cartoons and captions are, for me, an affectionate nudge at what we still are. Even if we don't change, we can laugh at our mistakes. Movements will come and go. Some to castrate men and some to rob women of their womanhood, but somewhere in there is a democracy of consideration where we may find an entirely lovable world . . .

I must be out of my mind!

MARCELLA MARKHAM

A male chauvinist thinks that, "Whither thou goest I will go", was said by a woman to a man

A chauvinist answers for you

A chauvinist is adorable to you when he has a high temperature

Chauvinists run away when you're sick

A chauvinist clumps on your feet and blames the music . . .

. . . a dear clumps on your feet, but he apologises

Chauvinists grope . . .

. . . men hold

Chauvinists pull in their tummies when a beautiful
beach girl walks by

Chauvinists are easy to be with – they're predictable

A chauvinist thinks Women's Liberation is taking you to a football match

A Chauvinist is...

A chauvinist keeps shouting, "Woman driver!" – mostly at young men

A chauvinist doesn't make out a will

A chauvinist writes to you as Mrs. Richard Smith

A chauvinist fights his wife's battles

A chauvinist talks about "the wife" and "the girlfriend"

Loving a chauvinist is identifying with your mother

Only chauvinists ask a woman director to take the minutes at a board meeting

A chauvinist *likes* board meetings

A chauvinist tells the truth about your new hairstyle

Chauvinists pinch bottoms

Chauvinists actually *wear* their M C P ties

A chauvinist admires your new dress just before he demolishes you in the boardroom

A chauvinist hates Germaine Greer – but thinks she's sexy

Nice mummies create chauvinists

A chauvinist says, "Why don't you get your hair done" when you arrive back from the hairdressers

A chauvinist says you look divine and then asks how much the dress cost him

A chauvinist looks proud when you give a perfect
dinner for the boss. . .

. . . and tells you you're "extravagant" when the boss has left

A chauvinist happily buys drinks all round but keeps checking your housekeeping money

A chauvinist is a big spender who tells you to buy
something special for yourself . . . and then doesn't pay

A chauvinist goes on about "my car" and "my house"
when you drive the first and clean the second

A married chauvinist has only his name on the door

Only chauvinists shout at waiters

A Chauvinist is . . .

A chauvinist thinks that when a woman says, "No", she really means, "Yes"

A chauvinist doesn't ask you if you are on the pill

A chauvinist doesn't bath before – or cuddle after

If a chauvinist can't make love, he'll tell you you lack 'frisson'

A rich chauvinist thinks giving you his money is more personal than giving his body

A chauvinist will use your body to use you

A chauvinist flirts with the baby-sitter

Chauvinists *can* turn you on but you resent every minute of it

A chauvinist wants to know if he is better than your previous lover

A chauvinist uses your flat and complains about the bed

A chauvinist says, "Me too," when you say, "I love you"

A chauvinist admires your new dress just before he pounces on it and you

Only a chauvinist asks his secretary to shop for his wife's present

A chauvinist asks all prospective women executives if
they can type

A chauvinist keeps pictures of his family all over the office while he chases you around his desk

A chauvinist is a fifteen stone bore who ogles girlie magazines

A chauvinist judge looks at a female and weighs her
re-marrying appeal

A banker is a chauvinist who doesn't believe a woman
can handle a mortgage

Chauvinists are macho-mechanics who offer to give
the full diagnosis to your husband

A chauvinist eats garlic – raw

Chauvinists assume that any woman dining alone is looking for a man

A chauvinist says he loves you, but loves himself

A chauvinist says his wife has given up cooking for him

A chauvinist tells you his wife is paralysed from the waist down

A chauvinist calls you "darling", "honey", "baby", *anything* except your name

A chauvinist loves himself so much he can't believe
you don't

A chauvinist doesn't shave before . . .

. . . and snores after

A chauvinist never phones you the day after (mean slob)

A Chauvinist is ...

When everyone admires your new dress, only a chauvinist tells them the price

A chauvinist is someone who gives you an allowance and then lets you ask for it each week

A chauvinist doesn't tell you how much he makes

A chauvinist hates you to work – but doesn't mind spending the money

A chauvinist is put out when you're too tired to cook when you get home from work

A chauvinist can easily afford double whiskies – but not piano lessons for his daughter

A chauvinist is bored by school plays and sports days

Chauvinists wear Bunny Club ties in front of their daughters

A female chauvinist is a chain smoker who complains about her husband's cigars

A dumb chauvinist complains that men "only want one thing" and doesn't realize that's all she has to offer

A female chauvinist never makes a man feel desirable

There are gross pigs and gross piggess's and they deserve each other

Chauvinists *can* be ladies

A woman chauvinist doesn't say "Thank you", when a
man opens the door for her

A female chauvinist can't wait to prove she's smarter than a man

A female chauvinist bitches about and at other women

A Chauvinist is...

A chauvinist tells you that you are a great suitcase packer so please will you do it for him

A chauvinist is an egocentric ass who won't learn to cook

A chauvinist leaves the toilet seat up

A chauvinist likes cotton sheets and cotton shirts (and can't iron)

All those detergent ads were made up by chauvinists

Chauvinists are late for Sunday lunch

You have to praise a chauvinist for helping in a crisis

A chauvinist is a cigar smoker who can't stand cooking smells

A chauvinist doesn't mind if supper is ten minutes late when you have 'flu

A chauvinist's wife won't take off for the weekend because she can't face a sink full of dirty dishes on Monday

The ultimate chauvinist stubs his cigarettes out on your carpet

Underneath every great chauvinist is a woman

A chauvinist tells you how pretty you look when you're angry

A chauvinist bellows at people but dismisses your
anger as "that time of the month"

A chauvinist can't apologize

Chauvinists are sure they know the way and won't
believe your map-reading until you're lost

A chauvinist has two endorsements and calls you his
"pretty little back-seat driver"

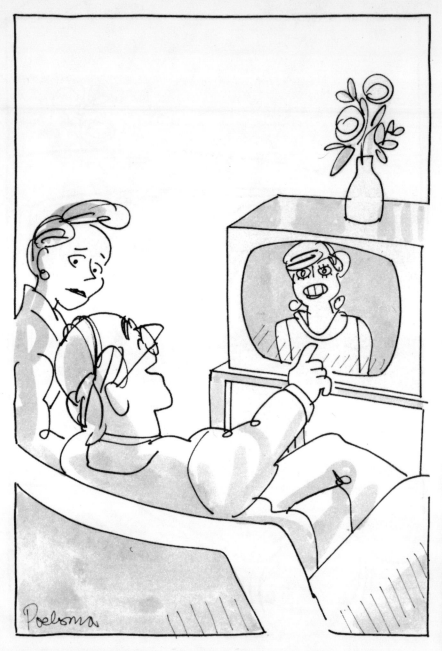

A chauvinist always criticises the teeth of a woman
newsreader . . .

. . . and never says, "That middle-aged, fat boozer",
when it's a man

A chauvinist watches you paint the room and points out your mistakes

A chauvinist is a brilliant engineer, who can't use a
washing machine

A chauvinist says, "Can I help you with the dishes?"
Then he falls asleep while you do them

A chauvinist sometimes offers to help with the
housework but misses the dust

A chauvinist gets a funny expression on his face when
you go near his hi-fi

A chauvinist is a father who can't change a nappy

All chauvinists are married to naggers

A chauvinist doesn't know where the teacups are – if he lives with you a lifetime

Some interesting ideas for presents

Grandmas and Grandpas, £3.95
Children are close to grandparents, and this reflects that warmth. 'A Grandma is old on the outside and young on the inside.' An endearing book for grandparents.

To Dad, £3.95
'Fathers are always right, and even if they're not right, they're never actually wrong.' Dads will love this book – it's so true to life! A regular favourite.

To Mum, £3.95
'When I'm sad she patches me up with laughter.' A thoughtful, joyous gift for mum, entirely created by children. Get it for Mother's Day or her birthday.

Here are other Exley books which make useful little gifts for birthdays, Mother's Day, anniversaries and Christmas. Simply order through your bookshop, or by post from Exley Publications Ltd, 12 Ye Corner, Chalk Hill, Watford, Herts, WD1 4BS. Please add 15p in the £ as a contribution to postage and packing.

Shopping by Post for Gardeners, £3.95
Here at last you can find who supplies unusual plants or equipment – and get them delivered to your door from anywhere in Britain. A super gift for the keen gardener.

Love, a celebration, £5.60
Writers and poets old and new have captured the feeling of being in love, in this very personal collection. Gift-wrapped with sealing wax. Give it to someone special.

Old is great! £3.25
A wicked book of cartoons which pokes fun at youth and revels in the first grey hairs of middle age. 'Extremely funny' *(Daily Telegraph)*. Also, by the same author, *A Chauvinist is* . . . £3.25

See Britain at Work, £5.95
Hundreds of glassworks, potteries, power stations, factories and craft workshops you can visit on your next holiday. Over 200 pages and over 150 illustrations. A valuable family reference book.

The Magic of London's Museums, £4.50
This illustrated guide to all London's Museums – almost 100 of them – provides endless ideas for your next visit to London. Ideal for parents, holiday makers and teachers.

What is a husband? £3.95
7500 real wives attempted to answer the question, and the best quotes are here. Pithy, beautiful, hilarious, sad, romantic – all you might expect. Buy a copy for your anniversary!

What is a baby? £3.95
Parents and grandparents describe the fun and traumas of bringing up baby. A hilarious and beautiful gift book for any young mother, stunningly illustrated with beautiful photographs.

Give Happiness a Chance, £4.95
Quiet, beautiful and sensitive. This book has swept Europe, with sales of one and a half million copies. A memorable and thoughtful gift, especially valued, perhaps, by someone who is lonely.